FRANCIS FRITH'S

WILMSLOW AND ALDERLEY EDGE

PHOTOGRAPHIC MEMORIES

Once a teacher at St Hilary's School, Alderley Edge, **CLARE PYE** works at the Manchester Museum on its joint research work with the National Trust, The Alderley Edge Landscape Project. A lecturer on local history for Keele University and at the Wilmslow Guild, she is a member of the National Trust's Alderley Edge Advisory Committee.

FRANCIS FRITH'S
PHOTOGRAPHIC MEMORIES

WILMSLOW AND ALDERLEY EDGE

PHOTOGRAPHIC MEMORIES

CLARE PYE

First published in the United Kingdom in 2004 by
Frith Book Company Ltd

Limited Hardback Subscribers Edition Published in 2004
ISBN 1-85937-855-2

Paperback Edition 2004
ISBN 1-85937-856-0

British Library Cataloguing in Publication Data

Francis Frith's Wilmslow and Alderley Edge -
Photographic Memories
Clare Pye

Frith Book Company Ltd
Frith's Barn, Teffont,
Salisbury, Wiltshire SP3 5QP
Tel: +44 (0) 1722 716 376
Email: info@francisfrith.co.uk
www.francisfrith.co.uk

Printed and bound in Great Britain

Front Cover: **WILMSLOW**, *Grove Street c1955* W103006
Frontispiece: **ALDERLEY EDGE**, *The Hough 1896* 37464

*The colour-tinting is for illustrative purposes only, and is not intended
to be historically accurate*

AS WITH ANY HISTORICAL DATABASE THE FRITH ARCHIVE IS
CONSTANTLY BEING CORRECTED AND IMPROVED AND THE
PUBLISHERS WOULD WELCOME INFORMATION ON OMISSIONS OR
INACCURACIES

CONTENTS

FRANCIS FRITH
VICTORIAN PIONEER

FRANCIS FRITH, founder of the world-famous photographic archive, was a complex and multi-talented man. A devout Quaker and a highly successful Victorian businessman, he was philosophical by nature and pioneering in outlook.

By 1855 he had already established a wholesale grocery business in Liverpool, and sold it for the astonishing sum of £200,000, which is the equivalent today of over £15,000,000. Now a very rich man, he was able to indulge his passion for travel. As a child he had pored over travel books written by early explorers, and his fancy and imagination had been stirred by family holidays to the sublime mountain regions of Wales and Scotland. 'What lands of spirit-stirring and enriching scenes and places!' he had written. He was to return to these scenes of grandeur in later years to 'recapture the thousands of vivid and tender memories', but with a different purpose. Now in his thirties, and captivated by the new science of photography, Frith set out on a series of pioneering journeys up the Nile and to the

Near East that occupied him from 1856 until 1860.

INTRIGUE AND EXPLORATION

These far-flung journeys were packed with intrigue and adventure. In his life story, written when he was sixty-three, Frith tells of being held captive by bandits, and of fighting 'an awful midnight battle to the very point of surrender with a deadly pack of hungry, wild dogs'. Wearing flowing Arab costume, Frith arrived at Akaba by camel sixty years before Lawrence of Arabia, where he encountered 'desert princes and rival sheikhs, blazing with jewel-hilted swords'.

He was the first photographer to venture beyond the sixth cataract of the Nile. Africa was still the mysterious 'Dark Continent', and Stanley and Livingstone's historic meeting was a decade into the future. The conditions for picture taking confound belief. He laboured for hours in his wicker dark-room in the sweltering heat of the desert, while the volatile chemicals fizzed dangerously in their trays. Back in London he exhibited his photographs and was 'rapturously cheered' by members of the Royal Society. His reputation as a photographer was made overnight.

VENTURE OF A LIFE-TIME

Characteristically, Frith quickly spotted the opportunity to create a new business as a specialist publisher of photographs. He lived in an era of immense and sometimes violent change.

For the poor in the early part of Victoria's reign work was exhausting and the hours long, and people had precious little free time to enjoy themselves. Most had no transport other than a cart or gig at their disposal, and rarely travelled far beyond the boundaries of their own town or village. However, by the 1870s the railways had threaded their way across the country, and Bank Holidays and half-day Saturdays had been made obligatory by Act of Parliament. All of a sudden the working man and his family were able to enjoy days out and see a little more of the world.

With typical business acumen, Francis Frith foresaw that these new tourists would enjoy having souvenirs to commemorate their days out. In 1860 he married Mary Ann Rosling and set out on a new career: his aim was to photograph every city, town and village in Britain. For the next thirty years he travelled the country by train and by pony and trap, producing fine photographs of seaside resorts and beauty spots that were keenly bought by millions of Victorians. These prints were painstakingly pasted into family albums and pored over during the dark nights of winter, rekindling precious memories of summer excursions.

THE RISE OF FRITH & CO

Frith's studio was soon supplying retail shops all over the country. To meet the demand he gathered about him a small team of photographers, and published the work of independent artist-photographers of the calibre of Roger Fenton and Francis Bedford. In order to gain some understanding of the scale of Frith's business one only has to look at the catalogue issued by Frith & Co in 1886: it runs to some 670 pages, listing not only many thousands of views of the British Isles but also many photographs of most European countries, and China, Japan, the USA and Canada - note the sample page shown on page 9 from the hand-written Frith & Co ledgers recording the pictures. By 1890 Frith had created the greatest specialist photographic publishing company in the world, with over 2,000 sales outlets - more than the combined number that Boots and WH Smith have today! The picture on the next page shows the Frith & Co display board at Ingleton in the Yorkshire Dales (left of window). Beautifully constructed with a mahogany frame and gilt inserts, it could display up to a dozen local scenes.

POSTCARD BONANZA

The ever-popular holiday postcard we know today took many years to develop. In 1870 the Post Office issued the first plain cards, with a pre-printed stamp on one face. In 1894 they allowed other publishers' cards to be sent through the mail with an attached adhesive halfpenny stamp. Demand grew rapidly, and in 1895 a new size of postcard was permitted called the court card, but there was little room for illustration. In 1899, a year after Frith's death, a new card measuring 5.5 x 3.5 inches became the standard format, but it was not until 1902 that the divided back came into being, so that the address and message could be on one face and a full-size illustration on the other. Frith & Co were in the vanguard of postcard development: Frith's sons Eustace and Cyril continued their father's monumental task, expanding the number of views offered to the public and recording more and more places in Britain, as the

coasts and countryside were opened up to mass travel.

Francis Frith had died in 1898 at his villa in Cannes, his great project still growing. The archive he created continued in business for another seventy years. By 1970 it contained over a third of a million pictures showing 7,000 British towns and villages.

FRANCIS FRITH'S LEGACY

Frith's legacy to us today is of immense significance and value, for the magnificent archive of evocative photographs he created provides a unique record of change in the cities, towns and villages throughout Britain over a century and more. Frith and his fellow studio photographers revisited locations many times down the years to update their views, compiling for us an enthralling and colourful pageant of British life and character.

We are fortunate that Frith was dedicated to recording the minutiae of everyday life. For it is this sheer wealth of visual data, the painstaking chronicle of changes in dress, transport, street layouts, buildings, housing, engineering and landscape that captivates us so much today. His remarkable images offer us a powerful link with the past and with the lives of our ancestors.

THE VALUE OF THE ARCHIVE TODAY

Computers have now made it possible for Frith's many thousands of images to be accessed almost instantly. Frith's images are increasingly used as visual resources, by social historians, by researchers into genealogy and ancestry, by architects and town planners, and by teachers involved in local history projects.

In addition, the archive offers every one of us an opportunity to examine the places where we and our families have lived and worked down the years. Highly successful in Frith's own era, the archive is now, a century and more on, entering a new phase of popularity. Historians consider the Francis Frith Collection to be of prime national importance. It is the only archive of its kind remaining in private ownership. Francis Frith's archive is now housed in an historic timber barn in the beautiful village of Teffont in Wiltshire. Its founder would not recognize the archive office as it is today. In place of the many thousands of dusty boxes containing glass plate negatives and an all-pervading odour of photographic chemicals, there are now ranks of computer screens. He would be amazed to watch his images travelling round the world at unimaginable speeds through internet lines.

The archive's future is both bright and exciting. Francis Frith, with his unshakeable belief in making photographs available to the greatest number of people, would undoubtedly approve of what is being done today with his lifetime's work. His photographs depicting our shared past are now bringing pleasure and enlightenment to millions around the world a century and more after his death.

WILMSLOW AND ALDERLEY EDGE
AN INTRODUCTION

SOUTH-WEST of Manchester is now comfortable commuting country; people live in north-eastern Cheshire and use the good transport links to get where they need to go. Their concerns are urban, even if they have escaped into suburbia, and their lives can be models of conspicuous consumption. A few years ago, an off-licence in Alderley Edge village sold more bottles of champagne in a year than anywhere else in the country. However, underneath this sparkling surface are the signs of an older rural society, and there is more of this heritage in the landscape than may first appear to the casual visitor.

The physical geography is varied, but overlooking the Cheshire Plain it is dominated by the rearing sandstone escarpment of Alderley Edge. South-east of the Edge is the undulating country of the dip slope, a well wooded and often private landscape of near horizons that can reveal unexpected surprises. Through the country on the north-east of the Edge winds the River Bollin and its tributary the Dean Water, both coming down from the Macclesfield hills to flow past the airport to the Mersey. The plain itself is flat, a mixture of clay, sand and occasionally peat.

The geology of the area influences the buildings. Even though there was relatively good building stone available from Alderley Edge for the more important buildings, such as churches, this was predominately a half-timbered countryside until bricks became available with the Industrial Revolution. The substantial farmhouses built during the 17th and 18th centuries testify to the prosperity of the Cheshire dairy industry, when its cheese was famous as far as the capital.

ALDERLEY EDGE, *The Liberal Club 1896* 37453

10

However, all this changed with the coming of the railways. Within 20 years, well-to-do commuter communities had sprung up along the lines; indeed, Alderley Edge village itself did not exist before the trains came - it is a Victorian creation dating from 10 May 1842, when the station opened. Other villages, such as Wilmslow and Prestbury, expanded to become the places they are today.

Yet, as one travels around, one meets pockets of very old landscape, and some places still exert the same fascination as they did hundreds of years ago. Lindow Moss, the peat bog shared between Wilmslow and Mobberley, is still in places the mysterious half-land half-water landscape where two thousand years ago a Celtic tribe sought to appease the gods and keep the Romans at bay by sacrificing one of the best of their warriors. Lindow Man reappeared in 1984, but he was not the first bog body to emerge out of the moss. A few years before, another head had been found, and so well preserved was it that the police treated it at first as a murder enquiry, and indeed arrested a man whose wife had recently disappeared. Faced with what he thought was the discovery of her body, he confessed and was convicted of murder.

Such bizarre episodes testify to the fact that this seemingly respectable landscape of well-to-do businessmen (together with the odd footballer and his wife) has a number of quirks. There are others. The flat landscape of Mobberley bred one of our country's most famous mountaineers, George Leigh Mallory. Beside the A34 in Nether Alderley is the grave of the third Lord Stanley, buried apart from the rest of his relations as he was a Muslim. Up on the Edge is the oldest-dated copper mine in England, and evidence that the Romans were looking for lead as soon as they conquered this part of the world, proof indeed that the sacrifices in nearby Lindow were in vain.

As befits a landscape with such a deep heritage, the National Trust has considerable parts of the area under its care, notably Alderley Edge, and Styal with its Mill, accompanying village and walks in the woods along the Bollin. Elsewhere concerned residents do their best to make sure that this landscape remains as unspoiled as possible, although the nearby Manchester Airport makes it clear that modern life cannot be kept completely at bay.

ALDERLEY EDGE, *Chapel Road c1955* A29011

ALDERLEY EDGE

ALDERLEY EDGE has been here since the last Ice Age. It is the sandstone escarpment above the Cheshire Plain, mined since the Early Bronze Age for its copper, treasured and landscaped by its owners the Stanleys of Alderley until they sold up in 1938, and now largely owned by the National Trust who manage this popular beauty spot for thousands of visitors. It has a legend, of sleeping soldiers under the hill and a farmer from Mobberley who supplied a horse for them in return for treasure.

Alderley Edge village below the hill is a much more recent creation, made by the coming of the railway in 1842, when it was decided to create the first up-market commuter suburb in the north-west. The very name of the village is a railway invention; the community lay in Chorley, one of Wilmslow's townships, but the developers did not want any confusion with Chorley in Lancashire,

so the name of the nearby hill was adopted. The neighbouring Stanleys of Alderley Park did not approve; for them, Alderley was the name of the separate parish to the south where they lived.

The middle-class villas up on the Edge and the service village below on the plain made a tightly-knit dependent community. In the 21st century, it is more homogenously middle-class as the property prices have rocketed, and the London Road, which within recent memory was a street of individually owned shops, is now in the process of redevelopment, with apartment blocks the key element. How the character of the village will change when the long awaited bypass arrives in a few years time is a question we cannot answer yet, but no doubt Alderley Edge village will continue to do what it has done since Victorian times, reinvent itself to suit a changing but always well-to-do society.

ALDERLEY EDGE
From the Railway Station 1896 37445

Looking up Trafford Road, one can see the large villas on the Edge, above the village that serviced their needs. On the corner is Tyler's garden nursery; Mr Tyler was ready to supply everything from a packet of seeds to a full landscaping service, on account, of course, to the suitable customer. Later, Alderley council offices occupied the site.

ALDERLEY EDGE
*The Railway Station
1896* 37446

Without the railway station, Alderley Edge village would not exist. It was planned as a wealthy commuter village in 1842 when the railway was built to meet the needs of the Lancashire businessmen who wanted to live away from the smoky industrial towns where they made their money. The aristocratic Stanleys of Alderley called them Railroadians or Cottentots.

ALDERLEY EDGE, *London Road 1896* 37447

This is now the busy A34, and the village will soon have a bypass. The traffic is often at a standstill, but it was once safe enough for children to stand in the middle of the road. The little gardens have gone, but the pavements are still wider than average, and, as the shops still own the space immediately in front, they continue to put out billboards.

▶ **ALDERLEY EDGE**
London Road 1896
37448

This view is looking north up Alderley Edge's main shopping street, the little gardens in front of the premises can clearly be seen. On the left is Bilsboroughs, smiths and ironmongers, a business that lasted from the 1860s to 1990s. On the right, the black and white building became the garage, Eadingtons. During the Second World War, Mrs Armitage, who had taken to using her pony and trap to save petrol, would tie the pony up to the pump when she came down to the village to shop, never mind the inconvenience to anyone else.

◀ **ALDERLEY EDGE**
London Road 1896
37450

Another view of the London Road reveals the Trafford Arms on the left, an unofficial club for the gardeners who worked in the villas. They gathered here at lunchtime, only dispersing when the local builders, Isaac Massey and Son, sounded its one o'clock hooter. In the background is the Institute, built by villa owners for St Philip's church to provide a respectable teetotal place for the villa maids to spend their weekly free afternoons.

◄ **ALDERLEY EDGE**
The Liberal Club 1896
37453

In the highly stratified society of Alderley Edge village, the Liberal Unionist Club in Stephen Street was for the village's tradesmen. It may have cost 5/- a year in 1896, but in the 1930s, the cost of membership had gone up to a pound a year, still beyond the reach of working men such as gardeners to become members. Besides the usual bar and bowling green, it boasted a library and reading room, and in the room above was Alderley's first cinema.

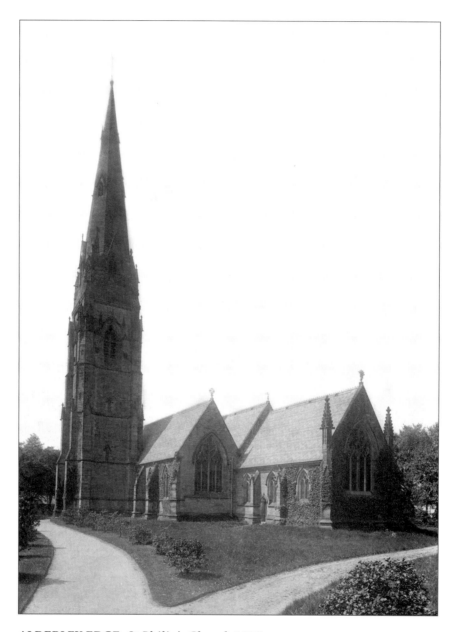

ALDERLEY EDGE, *St Philip's Church 1896* 37455

This church was designed by J S Crowther in 1853; the steeple tower and porch were added eleven years later. Class divisions were even found here; the morning service was for the villa families, and the evening service for the villagers. This pattern probably started because the villa servants could not go to church in the morning as they were cooking Sunday lunch for their employers.

ALDERLEY EDGE, *The Wesleyan Chapel 1896* 37457

Until Barclays Bank was built in 1904, the Methodist church had the only public clock in the village. Many of the Manchester businessmen that settled in Alderley in the mid 19th century came from a Nonconformist background and they often kept up their connections with the city. Miss Moxon would entertain Sunday schools from the Manchester slums in her garden at West Bank, and in the Second World War would always open her house to the evacuees no one else wanted.

▶ **ALDERLEY EDGE**
The Cottage Hospital c1955
A29002

Many people regretted the closure of Alderley Cottage Hospital a few years ago as it was very much part of the community, if only because of the number of tonsils that were extracted from local children over the years. Sometimes doctors here undertook more serious operations and one resident can remember having her appendix out - on D-Day!

◀ **ALDERLEY EDGE**
The Council Offices c1955 A29006

These offices were built just before the last war on the corner where Tyler's the nursery gardens had been in 1900, but they have now gone. During the Second World War this building was the headquarters for the ARP. Although Alderley Edge village itself was not hit, the German planes used to fly over the Edge 'and if they turned right they were going to Manchester, and if they went straight on, they were going to Liverpool', remembers one resident.

▲ **ALDERLEY EDGE,** *Rileys Lane c1955* A29009

At the junction of Rileys Lane and the A34 are St Philip's Parish Church and the Alderley Edge village war memorial. The latter is at the spiritual heart of the community, beside the church where many of the men worshipped. It is close to the lane that goes down to the village school, and faces one of the entrances to the railway station from where these men departed forever.

◄**ALDERLEY EDGE**
Duke Street c1960
A29030

The Victorian villas on the Edge can clearly be seen at the end of the road and across the field, then known as Lifeless Moss. When Marlborough Road was built in the 1960s, although it appears on a map to extend Duke Street towards the hill and one can walk through, there is no vehicular access between the two roads, so Duke Street remains a quiet back street in Alderley.

▼ **ALDERLEY EDGE,** *Windermere Drive 1966* A29043

This photograph was taken just after Windermere Drive was built, and St Philip's Church can be seen in the distance. Nearly 40 years later, everything is much more mellow now, as trees and shrubs have grown up. Seeing the initial bleakness of the estate, one can understand why these sixties developments were not universally welcomed at the time.

▶ **ALDERLEY EDGE**
London Road c1965
A29047

Even in the 1960s it was possible to park the car easily along the side of the road, although waiting restrictions had already been introduced. In the 1930s, there were seven butchers and ten grocers in the village, nearly all of them individual family shops. Most of them have gone now; however, Weinholts' the confectioners is still here, baking at the back and open only on Thursday, Friday and Saturday.

◄ **ALDERLEY EDGE**
Chorley Hall 1896
37470

The oldest secular building in the Alderley area, Chorley Hall was started in the 14th century, when moated manor houses were at the height of fashion. The half-timbered wing was added in the 16th century, just before it was bought by the Stanleys. In 1896, as the chickens and water pump testify, the Hall was still a working farmhouse.

▶ **ALDERLEY EDGE**
The Edge and the Hough 1896 37462

This photograph was probably taken from the railway line which gives a good view of the Edge across The Hough. Wood Hill and the Castle Rock viewpoint to its right can clearly be seen, with the Hough road to Mottram St Andrew at its foot. The swing boats in the field outside the cottage were in use every weekend when day trippers came out from Manchester.

21

◄ **ALDERLEY EDGE**
The Hough 1896
37464

The road through the Hough towards Wilmslow snakes into the murky distance, while in the foreground are the swing boats in the field of the cottage, a favourite venue for Sunday school outings. The barns of Finlow Bower farm, so called after Richard Finlow, a tenant in the 18th century, can be seen on the right. In 1896, they were offering refreshments to the day trippers to the Edge.

◀ **ALDERLEY EDGE**
The Edge 1896 37463

With the Hough on the left and looking towards Waterfall and Clockhouse Woods, the path up the Edge, originally an old right of way from the Hough over to Macclesfield, has recently been rebuilt by the National Trust. However, the erosion below Pillar Mine was too great for this restored path to follow the old line and it now has to twist and turn to reach the top of the crest.

◀ **ALDERLEY EDGE**
The Wizard Inn 1896
37452

Built in the 1780s as the Miners' Arms, this premises changed its name to the Wizard Inn in 1843. Lady Stanley, viewing the new sign, hoped that people would not 'mistake it for My Lord in his dressing gown'. When the third Lord Stanley inherited his title in 1869, being a Muslim, he closed all the public houses on his land. However, he allowed the Wizard to reopen as a teetotal tearoom for the many visitors who came to walk on the Edge.

ALDERLEY EDGE, *The Beacon 1896* 37465

Sited on a Bronze Age tumulus, the Beacon was built in Elizabethan times and was used at the time of the Armada to warn of the Spanish threat. The extra bricks and the conical top were improvements added by Sir John Stanley in the late 18th century. Unfortunately, the Beacon fell down during as storm in the 1930s, and was replaced by a simple memorial plaque.

ALDERLEY EDGE
The Stone Table of the Wizard 1896 37466

Looking at this photograph of the Druids' Stones, with the horizontal stone on top, one can understand why an early 19th-century antiquarian wanted to claim it as an Ancient British cromlech. However, the Hon Louisa Stanley had great pleasure in disabusing him, as she was only too well aware that it was part of her family's early 19th-century landscaping on the Edge. He was not made happy by this information.

ALDERLEY EDGE, *The Wizard's Well 1896* 37467

The path from the village to the Edge passes by the Wizard's Well, a 19th-century tourist attraction. Below the head carved above the well is an inscription which says, 'Drink of this and take thy fill, for the water falls by the Wizard's will.' On Victorian Bank Holidays, this path would be thronged, and the lone pipe-smoking man would have had little solitude to contemplate the Legend of Alderley Edge.

ALDERLEY EDGE
The Holy Well 1896
37468

The Holy Well is probably the oldest known well on the Edge. It may have been created in 1740, when two overhanging stones fell down the hill, making the houses in the Hough shake, and, according to legend, squashing an old woman and her cow. The well had the reputation of curing barrenness in women, and offerings of bent pins were sometimes left there.

ALDERLEY EDGE, *Keeper's Cottage 1896* 37479

This was the Stanley's game-keeper's cottage on Alderley Edge, built in 1837 by Sir John and Maria Stanley, according to the plaque in the gable. When the railway opened and day trippers flocked to Alderley, visitors to the Wizard Woods had to go through the wicket gate on the right to get admission to the Edge.

▲ **ALDERLEY EDGE,** *West Mine 1896*
37480

This great open-cast canyon no longer exists,
it was filled in by tipping household waste in
the 1960s, but it shows how active the
Alderley Edge Mining Company was in the
second quarter of the 19th century. Alderley
Edge is possibly the earliest site of copper
mining in England, as traces of Early Bronze
Age activity was proved by the Manchester
University's excavation here in 1997.

◄ *detail from 37480*

ALDERLEY EDGE, *West Mine 1896* 37481

When one looks at this inviting cavern, it is no wonder that after the copper mining itself finished West Mine became a magnet for explorers despite, or perhaps because of, the dangers of going underground. Between the two world wars Jack Perrin, who lived in the nearby Hagg Cottages, used to sit by the entrance and sell half candles to people who wanted to go down the mine.

ALDERLEY EDGE
*The View from
Castle Rock c1955*
A29013

This photograph is looking north over the Hough where Manchester's murk still obscures the horizon. Before clean air acts and the decline of the cotton industry, the only time people could see the Lancashire hills across the Mersey Basin was during Wakes week. Now the view is clearer, and any fine day will give a view across to Winter Hill and the Pennines.

ALDERLEY EDGE, *Castle Rock c1955* A29014

These girls look as if they are taking a break in their lunch hour, perhaps from the newly established ICI pharmaceutical laboratories in Alderley Park. However, looking out over the Bollin valley, they are doing no more than Mesolithic hunters did six or seven thousand years ago, as the flint remains nearby testify.

ALDERLEY EDGE, *The Wizard's Well c1955* A29016

The well is still a favourite spot to pause on the walk up the Edge from the village, one wonders if these are two prototypes of the children from Alan Garner's 'Weirdstone of Brisingamen', a 1960s reworking of the Alderley legend.

ALDERLEY EDGE
The Holy Well c1955
A29019

The wells on the Edge are dripping wells rather than bubbling springs. The water seeps out above an impermeable clay bed. Although the odd drink might not cause harm, as thirsty dogs can testify, the high mineral content, including lead and cobalt, means that the water is not fit to drink.

ALDERLEY EDGE, *Stormy Point c1955* A29021

This is another viewpoint on the Edge, from which it is usually possible to see the Cage in Lyme Park. The stone platform on the left has a memorial plaque on it to the Misses Pilkington, whose efforts in the 1940s ensured the Wizard Woods were saved from development and handed over to the National Trust in 1948. Erosion is now a problem here, and the Trust sometimes fences off areas to give a chance for the vegetation to regrow.

ALDERLEY EDGE
The Wizard c1955
A29024

By the time this photograph was taken, the Wizard had started its transformation from a cheerful tearoom for walkers and cyclists into a select restaurant. There were even plans in the early seventies to convert the outbuildings at the back into an 11-bedroom hotel. This did not happen, but the Wizard still does not have a full licence, a relic of its teetotal days.

NETHER ALDERLEY

OF ALL the villages in this collection, Nether Alderley perhaps gives us the best impression of what a north-eastern Cheshire village was like before the Industrial Revolution changed both the countryside and society. It still has an ancient church, a working mill and a collection of farmhouses along roads and lanes that have changed very little in the last 200 years.

Yet, once the proposed Alderley Edge bypass is built, the whole atmosphere will change as the road is planned to sweep through the calm countryside to the west of St Mary's church and across the drive of Heawood Hall.

However, when one looks under the surface, it is clear that much has already changed. The aristocratic landowners, the Stanleys of Alderley, sold up in 1938, and their park is now occupied by the research facilities for the pharmaceutical firm, Astra Zeneca. The Stanleys' one time care for their estate is still evident in their buildings in the village, often decorated with their crest, the Eagle and Child. They were an extraordinary family, witty and intellectual, who could count Bertrand Russell, Gertrude Bell and the Mitford sisters amongst their relations. But they have gone; a double dose of death duties and an extravagant sixth Lord Stanley meant they could not afford to continue living on the estates they had owned since the 15th century.

NETHER ALDERLEY
The Church 1896 37471

St Mary's in Nether Alderley is the oldest church in the Alderley area, and the nave dates from soon after the parish was created in 1300. The tower dates from the early 16th century, and was probably built by the same mason who built Mobberley church tower. The upper part of the two-storey feature is the Stanley pew, only reachable from the outside staircase on the right. Underneath the great yew tree on the far right is the grave of Mary Stanley, daughter of a rector of Alderley and one of Florence Nightingale's nurses in the Crimea.

NETHER ALDERLEY
The Church and the Rectory 1896 37474

This view across the fields towards St Mary's and its rectory can still be seen today from the public footpaths that go from the church to Gatley Farm and Sand Lane. It has been like this for 200 years, and almost a century before this photograph was taken the rector, the Rev Edward Stanley, painted a watercolour from almost exactly the same position.

NETHER ALDERLEY, *The Church, the Interior 1896* 37475

This was taken not long after the restoration of the interior of the church by the Reverend Bell. Very much in the Arts and Crafts style, each pew end is different, and the rector himself is remembered in a Morris window in the chancel. From an earlier era is the Stanley pew up above on the right, overlooking the pulpit like a Jacobean opera box. The Stanley crest of the Eagle and Child can just be seen above it. Today, below the pew, both a 'breeches' and a 'vinegar' bible are on show for visitors to see.

◄**NETHER ALDERLEY**
The Old Mill 1896 37478

At this time, Nether Alderley water mill was still the estate mill for the Stanley estate. The building we see here is largely Elizabethan; we know from the local records that it was 'new-builded' in 1597, but archaeologists have now worked out that some of the internal timbers date back to the 14th century. The mill pond behind the dam is also the moat for the Old Hall, where the Stanleys lived before a disastrous fire in 1779. However, water power can be unreliable, so the shed on the left with the chimney housed a steam engine to power the machinery if the water was too low.

◄ **NETHER ALDERLEY**
The Rectory 1896
37476

This rectory for many years was the home of the Reverend Edward Stanley, brother of the first Lord Stanley. A naturalist and most enlightened clergyman, when he was made Bishop of Norwich in 1838, he went round to say goodbye to all his parishioners. On his return as he dismounted his old horse collapsed and died, and is buried in the garden. Also in the garden is a very early specimen of a scarlet rhododendron, reputedly planted in Waterloo year, 1815.

◄ **NETHER ALDERLEY**
The Old Mill c1955
N148001

This is the mill in its derelict state before John Shelmardine presented it to the National Trust, and Dr Cyril Bouchier of UMIST started restoring the mill machinery to working order. The mill is unusual in that it has one water wheel above the other, so the mill increases the power it gets from the same water before it flows away under the A34 to the fields beyond St Mary's church. Inside on the walls are carved the initials of many of the millers, including the last from the 1930s, John Rawlins.

NETHER ALDERLEY
The Old School c1955
N148003

Built in St Mary's churchyard in the late 17th century with an endowment from Thomas Deane de Parke, this building educated the village boys until early last century. The schoolroom was below and the master lived above. On the far right is part of the extension to the school built in 1817 by the rector, the Rev Edward Stanley. When the boys moved out, the whole building became the parish hall.

NETHER ALDERLEY, *Potts' Shop c1955* N148006
Mr and Mrs Potts kept the village shop opposite the mill and on the corner of the A34 and Church Lane. In the 1930s, they also sold day licences for fishing in Radnor Mere in Alderley Park. The half-timbered house beyond used to be the village pub, the Eagle and Child, before the Muslim third Lord Stanley closed it in the early 1870s.

▲ **NETHER ALDERLEY**
The Cross 1896 37482

This view, looking north along what is now the main A34 towards Alderley Edge village, shows where Welsh Row crossed the old turnpike, connecting the old enclosed fields on the plain with the open common land of the Edge. At the crossroads is the stump of a cross, a reminder that in the 13th century, the then lord of the manor, Sir Walklyn Arderne, attempted but failed to found a market town here.

◄ *detail from 37482*

◀ **NETHER ALDERLEY**
Artists' Lane 1896 37460

On the old maps, this is Upper Welsh Row a continuation of the lane on the other side of the crossroads. When Alderley Edge was common land, the villagers' animals would be taken up this road to graze on the top of the hill. Further up at Butts Farm was the village pound to hold stray animals. The cottages on the right have narrow gardens running along the road, characteristic of squatters' cottages squeezed in on the verge between the road and the fields.

◄ NETHER ALDERLEY
Welsh Row 1896 37459

Looking East along Welsh Row towards the cross, this is Nut Tree Farm, a typical yeoman half timbered farmhouse from the 17th century. It has the characteristic north Cheshire coving under the gable. After this picture was taken a new wing was built on the far side, brick, but painted to match the rest of the house, and ornamented with the Stanley crest in the gable, a common feature of Stanley estate building at this time.

◄ NETHER ALDERLEY
Heawood Hall 1896 37486

Heawood Hall was a small gentry house in Nether Alderley, once the home of the Hollinsheds, a family that included the 16th-century chronicler who was Shakespeare's source for many of his history plays. The Stanleys bought the house in the early 19th century and it was split into two. The back was occupied by a farmer, while the front housed a flourishing girls' school run by the Misses Bell, sisters to Nether Alderley's rector.

NETHER ALDERLEY
The Smithy in
Bradford Lane 1896
37477A

The long leather aprons are
still characteristic of the
smith's trade, protecting the
workers from the horses'
hooves and the sparks from
the hot shoes. This is no
lumbering farm Shire horse
needing shoeing by Joseph
Worthington, but a smart
riding horse, perhaps a
Stanley hack from Alderley
Park.

CHELFORD

CHELFORD is better known as a village that is passed through rather than a destination in itself for it stands on an important crossroads, where the route between Manchester and the Midlands crosses the Knutsford to Macclesfield road. Consequently, when the railway was built from Manchester to Crewe, it had an important railway station, for, until the Macclesfield and Knutsford lines were both built about 20 years later, the stage coaches still had to come out to Chelford from those two towns to link up with the London train. Not surprisingly, a flourishing livestock market grew up here and, in the last 50 years, other transport firms have made Chelford their base and more markets have developed in the area.

So, it is a village that presents a rather reserved face to the world, and the heavy traffic quartering the village makes it difficult to pinpoint a centre. The church is opposite the entrance to Astle Park, some way from the station and shops, and the Dixon Arms, which used to provide a focal point, has recently been demolished to make way for yet more residential development, whose chief attraction will probably be the ease with which future residents can leave the place.

CHELFORD
Astle Hall 1896 37487

This rather severe Neo Classical house was built for Thomas Parker, whose family were squires of Chelford in the 18th and early 19th century. Its Wyatt origins can be seen in the plainness of the façade and the end windows, so reminiscent of Tatton Park. Thomas Parker had no children, so the estate passed to his sister's family, the Dixons.

CHELFORD
Astle Hall Lake 1896
37488

One of the most attractive features of Astle Park was the lake, now almost silted up. When the park was being created at the end of the 18th century, Roman remains were found, and there has always been a suspicion that a Roman road runs through the area, although this idea has never been confirmed. However, from its name, the nearby Pepper Street suggests a Roman route.

CHELFORD, *The Church 1896* 37489

Dedicated to St John the Evangelist, the main part of the church was built at the Parkers' expense at the end of the 18th century, but the tower is an 1840s addition by their successors the Dixons. Inside, there are pleasant Arts and Crafts features, including some late Morris and Co windows.

CHELFORD
Old Cottages c1955
C461003

At first glance, Church
Houses seem to be typical
farm labourers' cottages
next door to the church, but
a closer look at the left-
hand group suggests that
once this was a single
substantial farmhouse.
The clues lie in the half
timbering at the far end and
the substantial detailed
gables suggesting its once
higher status.

◀ **CHELFORD**
The Parish Room
c1955 C461008

Chelford is a village of markets. There is the long established weekly livestock market by the station; this has now been joined by a Sunday market, and just out of the village there is a flourishing car boot sale venue. The Parish Room or Village Hall is the place for antique markets, exhibitions and village shows

◄ **CHELFORD**
The Roundabout c1955
C461005

This is where the road
between Knutsford and
Macclesfield crosses the one
from Alderley Edge village to
Holmes Chapel. Now a busy
commuter intersection, the
street furniture has changed.
However, the village post
office on the opposite side
of the roundabout is still
there, although instead of
Hovis, it now advertises the
National Lottery.

◄ **CHELFORD**
Macclesfield Road c1955
C461013

The Macclesfield road rises in
the distance to the bridge over
the railway line, with the station
and livestock market going down
on the left. The Westminster
Bank and the Dixon Arms were
both there to serve the farmers
who came to the market.
The pub has recently been
demolished, but it had a late
hour of glory during the 1997
General Election, when it was
besieged by the nation's press as
inside, the local Conservatives
deliberated whether to back Neil
Hamilton as their candidate for
the Knutsford seat.

HENBURY

Henbury, or to give it its full title, Henbury cum Pexhill, is often overshadowed by its big neighbour, Macclesfield, and seen as an outlier to the town on the road to Knutsford. Quiet undulating wooded countryside is its main characteristic, especially on the Pexhill side of the community. The village is now best known for its flourishing garden centre and for the horse trials at Henbury Hall, where Julian Bicknall recently built a miniature Palladian Villa Rotunda for Basil de Ferranti.

HENBURY, *The Church 1897* 40467

Henbury was not a parish until 1845; before then it was part of Prestbury, so St Thomas' Church and its parsonage date from this time. The money was provided by the Marslands, who then lived at Henbury Hall, and Richard Lane did the designs. The church was sited on the main road, convenient for reforming Broken Cross, then an area of evil reputation. It is quite simple in design, stone with lancet windows.

MOBBERLEY

TO THE modern visitor, Mobberley appears to be strung out along Town Lane between Alderley and Knutsford, with at least three centres to the village. There is the modern settlement by the Ilford Works, two communities either side of the Mobberley Brook, and a cluster of houses by the Bird in Hand.

It is only when one looks at the history of the place that one gets a clue as to what is going on. Since the Middle Ages, Mobberley has not had a dominant landowner resident in the village. Instead, in the early 17th century there was a tenants' buyout from a couple of non-resident landowners. There is nothing like multiple land ownership to set the landscape as it is virtually impossible to effect any large-scale rearrangement on which everyone will agree. It helps to explain that, except for the post war development, Mobberley is a village of many pubs, as each little settlement knot has at least one place of refreshment.

The other factor, which again is not immediately apparent, is the influence of Lindow Moss on the village. Every freeholder in Mobberley had rights to cut peat from the Moss, usually in their designated 'moss rooms' or narrow strips of peaty land. This means that even in the 20th century each smallholding was divided between the meadow land around the main farmstead and the moss room on Lindow.

Nowadays, one of the main features of the village is the air traffic overhead. Not long ago, no house was complete without a sign against building a second runway at Manchester Airport, and respectable matrons made common cause with dreadlocked eco-warriors. All was unavailing, the runway was built and the planes roar above the village.

MOBBERLEY, *The Church 1903* 49687

Originally a community of canons, St Wilfrid's Church has served the people of Mobberley for 700 years. The tower was built in the early 16th century, as the inscription round it says. We even know the name of the stone-mason, Richard Plat. Inside there is a window dedicated to the memory of the Himalayan climber, George Leigh Mallory, whose family came from the village.

MOBBERLEY
The Victory Hall
c1955 M238007

Built after the First World War as part of the village's memorial to the men who fought in the conflict, standing above the Mobberley Brook and the main road through the village, the hall is still very much the centre of village life.

MOBBERLEY, *Mill Lane c1955* M238009

The creeper-covered wall between the iron fence and the cottage gable is in fact the dam wall for the mill. Now a silted up boggy patch, the mill pond can still be made out. To the right, Spout Lane goes round to the other side of the village; as the name suggests it is another watery place and there is still a spring that can be reached down some steps from beside the roadway.

▼ **MOBBERLEY,** *The Bird in Hand c1955* M238011

Because of its history of divided land ownership, it is difficult to determine the real centre of Mobberley village, but each nucleus has at least one inn. The Bird in Hand is the most easterly of four old public houses serving the community. Out of sight to the right is an old chapel so people feeling the need to repent, or to drown their sorrows, did not have far to go.

▶ **MOBBERLEY**
Town Lane c1960
M238015

In the 1950s and early 1960S, Mobberley saw an increase in housing, this time by a mixture of local authority and private development. This is a typical parade of local shops intended to give the housewife access to all that she might need for her family, before the days of deep freezers and universal motor transport. The corner shop, selling groceries, sweets and tobacco would provide for most of her wants.

◄ MOBBERLEY
The Ilford Works
c1960 M238018

On the opposite side of the road from the parade of shops is the Ilford works, built to develop everyone's holiday film, and with a wartime history of processing the films brought back by aircraft reconnaissance to Ringway. Later it turned to concentrating on specialist photographic services. The buildings by the road have been sold off recently and the land, like so much in Mobberley, is being developed for housing.

► MOBBERLEY
Slade Lane c1960
M238020

This peaceful unassuming lane crossing the brook is typical of the quiet countryside that has now gone with the expansion of Manchester Airport. One or two listed buildings were saved, dismantled and erected elsewhere, but the general character of the area has been transformed.

PRESTBURY

The name Prestbury, or Priest's Town, tells us all about its origins. It was the centre of an enormous parish, one of the biggest in England, and at the time of the Domesday Survey was one of the few villages in Cheshire to have its own priest. In the churchyard, there is a restored Norman-doored oratory, and the church itself, like many of the important churches in Cheshire, is entered through the impressive West Tower.

One of the reasons why the Church might have chosen this spot for its local headquarters may be because it is by an easy crossing over the River Bollin. Nowadays, at least since the coming of the railways in the 1860s, Prestbury has developed into a commuter suburb for Stockport and Manchester. Most of the development took place between the wars, by which time everyone respected the traditional architecture in the village, which helps to explain why the main street does not look so very different from 100 years ago.

PRESTBURY, *The Village 1896* 37438

Looking up the main street in Prestbury, the view 100 years ago seems to reveal a very similar dapper look to the one the village has today, although then there was no need for the extensive traffic calming measures that have just made their appearance in the village. Most of the houses on the right were still private houses.

▲ **PRESTBURY**
The High Street 1896 37439

Taken the same day as photograph 37438 (page 56) (note the ladder), this end of Prestbury seems much less kept than the view the other way. However, most of the buildings have not changed, although many of them are small shops rather than private houses.

◀ *detail from 37439*

PRESTBURY, *Red House 1896* 37440

This handsome 17th-century half-timbered house opposite the church was once the rectory for the enormous Prestbury parish. Besides the smart façade, one can also see the side wall, with enough evidence in the timber work to suggest that once the building was lower, and the attic floors are a later addition.

PRESTBURY
The Church 1896
37441

St Peter's Church in Prestbury has always been an important local church. Inside the largely 15th-century building, beside memorials to the lords of the manor, the Leghs of Adlington, there are early 18th-century wall paintings in the spandrels between the piers, depicting both the 12 apostles and the 12 tribes of Israel.

PRESTBURY, *The Manor House 1903* 49474

At the bottom of the street is the bridge over the River Bollin and the Manor house. Although the front betrays its 19th-century restoration, take a step back and one can see the complex Tudor chimneys of the original manor house. At the back the owners have recently found the remains of an Elizabethan knot garden, further proof of the house's ancient origins.

▶ PRESTBURY

Heeley Hall c1950 P111022

Prestbury inhabitants have often been careful of their privacy, and Heeley Hall is an example of the discrete country houses for which Prestbury is well known, and the immaculate grounds are typical of the type.

▼ PRESTBURY

Mottram Cross c1955 P111016

Although Mottram Cross has been moved back into the trees to allow the main road to be widened, it is still there, marking a once important crossroads. Priest Lane comes up from Mottram St Andrew and Alderley, and, transforming itself into a right of way along Smithy Lane, the route crosses over the main road to go behind the car and on over the Bollin towards Adlington and Stockport.

▶ PRESTBURY

The Old Admiral Rodney c1950 P111025

Just over the Bollin Bridge from the church, the Admiral Rodney is still dispensing hospitality, and ices can still be obtained from the next building, providing one sits down and has a full meal, as it is now one of the village's many restaurants.

◀ **PRESTBURY**
The Village c1950
P111026

The view down the street in 1950 is not greatly different from 50 years before, although a car has replaced the pony and trap. A sign of the growing commercialisation of the street can be seen in the Red House's transformation to the District Bank, and the private house beyond has become a high class decorator. Just beyond the churchyard and the Belisha beacon is the Bridge Hotel, still a popular restaurant and hotel.

HANDFORTH

Handforth used to nestle comfortably south of Cheadle and Bramhall and north of Wilmslow, but in the years since the Second World War it has become fully incorporated into Manchester suburbia, its proximity to the airport a key factor in its development, as the planes demonstrate when they fly low overhead.

However, farther back in its history we find the Hondford family who owned the manor. Their prosperous life ended with the death of William Hondford at the Battle of Flodden in 1513. One usually connects this battle with the deaths on the losing Scottish side and one can forget that this English victory was at the expense of many men from Cheshire, especially those who served in the companies of bowmen who were such an important part of the English army at this time. William's heiress was his daughter Margaret, and this is how the manor came into the possession of her husband Urian Brereton.

Military affairs came again to touch Handforth life more than a century later, as it was Urian Brereton's great grandson, Sir William, who was the Parliamentary commander in the Civil War. His son Thomas had no children and the estate was later rented out, so that the Hall became a farmhouse.

Now, Handforth is distinguished not so much by its past as by its present role as a commuter suburb to Manchester and Stockport and the out-of-town retail developments along the A34 bypass. What effects these latest changes will have on Handforth's character has yet to be fully worked out.

HANDFORTH, *The Hall c1960* H322007

Handforth Hall is a typical example of the 16th-century half-timbered manor houses in north-east Cheshire. The inscription above the porch tells the story: 'This haulle was buyilded in the year of oure lord God MCCCCCLXII by Uryan Brereton, knight, whom married Margaret, daughter and heyre of William Handforth Esquyer and had issue VI sonnes and II daughters.'

HANDFORTH

HANDFORTH
The Main Road c1965
H322014

This view of the shops in Handforth, taken from across the main Manchester Road shows a typical post-war development. Handforth expanded greatly after the Second World War with the influx of commuter housing, and the shopping parade was built to serve this. Many of the businesses are still local and the Esso garage at the end is one of the few signs of international commerce.

HANDFORTH, *Skyscraper Flats c1965* H322016

Typical of the Manchester overspill housing in the Handforth area, these system-built flats were thought to be the way forward in the 1960s. Only after families tried to live in them did their disadvantages become obvious.

HANDFORTH
The Greyhound Inn and High Street c1965
H322020

Looking south down the main road towards Wilmslow, with the road over to Macclesfield going off to the left, affluent Cheshire is driving towards the viewer and the young couple wait for the bus from Manchester to arrive. While Dales the cycles supplier may have been founded in 1903, its days as a business are numbered.

STYAL

To go to Styal now, it takes some imagination to see this place as a prime example of cutting edge technology, but 200 years ago this was the case. Now owned by the National Trust, it is a remarkable survival of one of the first stages of the Industrial Revolution, when the new water-powered mills had to seek fast-flowing streams to power their machinery.

Consequently these mills were often in isolated areas, and the owners had to create a complete infrastructure to support their industry. So, they had to build attractive housing within easy walking distance of work, and provide shops and places of worship. All this can be seen at Styal, which nestles in the steep sided wooded valley of the River Bollin, now welcoming hordes of visitors, especially school children, who come to experience what it was like to be a child worker and to see the mill still producing cotton cloth by water power.

STYAL, *The Cotton Mill 1897* 39616

Now owned by the National Trust, this is one of the best examples of a water powered cotton mill from the early years of the Industrial Revolution. It was extended over the years and the earliest part, dating from 1784, is the right hand section with the pediment and cupola. In the gable is the factory clock, and any employee late for work was fined. In the days before Greenwich Mean Time, this clock reigned supreme over everybody's life in Styal.

STYAL
*The Unitarian Chapel
1897* 39618

Like many businessmen in the 18th century the Gregs, who built Styal Mill, were Nonconformist, in their case Unitarians, and this was their chapel. Looking at their family tree, one can see how the Gregs were connected to many other important inventors and industrialists of the time, including Josiah Wedgwood and the Darbies of Coalbrookdale. Networking was as important 200 years ago as it is today.

STYAL, *The Village 1897* 39617

By the chapel is this village that the Gregs built for their workers. In the late 18th century, owners often had to attract workers to what were then quite remote parts of the countryside, and decent housing was one way to do it. The village had its own shop, farm and pub, where the Gregs kept a paternalistic eye on their workers' drinking habits. Between the village and the mill was the Apprentice House, where pauper children were housed, receiving their keep and training in return for working in the mill.

WILMSLOW

Technically, Wilmslow was just the parish church and its immediate graveyard, however, the name is now given to the whole of the community. The original lords of the manor were the Fittons, then the Venables inherited the land and, in the 15th century, the two Venables heiresses each took their half of the estates to their husband's family, the Booths of Dunham Massey and the Traffords of Trafford Park. Until the railway came in 1842 it was an isolated rural community, best known for its fustian and for its cottage industry making silk buttons for the Macclesfield silk industry. There was even a cotton mill in the middle of the town in the late 18th century, owned by the Bowen family.

However, once the trains came, Wilmslow became a thriving commuter community; its development hastened when the Earls of Stamford sold their land outright in the 1850s. This led to far fewer restrictions on building than in the neighbouring Alderley Edge, where strict leasehold conditions limited the development to select up-market residences.

One of the purchasers of the Stamford lands was J C Prescott, who bought up the old Bowen mill with its tall chimney and demolished it; he wanted to develop Wilmslow's residential potential and forget its industrial past. So, Wilmslow became a thriving mixed community and the shopping centre for the whole area; more of a town than a village.

In the last few years, with the building of the bypass round the town and its attendant retail development in Handforth, Wilmslow's shops have suffered, and the full extent of the impact of these changes has yet to be worked out.

WILMSLOW, *The Church from the South-West 1896* 37483

The origins of St Bartholomew's Church can be seen in its 14th-century crypt, but it was rebuilt in the 16th century when Henry Trafford was rector. Much of its present appearance owes a lot to the various restorations it went through in the 19th century, especially by J S Crowther in 1878.

WILMSLOW
*The Church from
the South 1896*
37484

This photograph was taken before the clerestory was added to the chancel by Bodley in 1898. He was a well known Liverpool architect, responsible for building Sunlight Village on the other side of the county in the Arts and Crafts style, although the Morris and Co windows in the church, dating from 1920, are too late to be his responsibility.

WILMSLOW, *The Church, the Interior 1896* 37485

The original lower height of the chancel roof can easily be seen, but otherwise, the interior is very similar to today's church. The chancel screen incorporates some 15th-century work, and the side chapels, as one might expect for a church at the centre of a large parish, used to belong to the prominent gentry families in the area, such as the Traffords and the Booths, both of whom married Venables heiresses in the 15th century and thus acquired large parts of Wilmslow. There is also a memorial to J C Prescott, one of Wilmslow's most important 19th-century developers.

WILMSLOW
*The Parish Church
c1955* W103002

The 1898 addition of a clerestory to the chancel can easily be seen here, as can the painted notice on the churchyard wall indicating that to the right it was 70 yards to a water supply, a leftover from ARP precautions in the Second World War more than 10 years before.

◄ **WILMSLOW**
The War Memorial c1955
W103011

This restrained war memorial was erected after the first war and added to after the second. It is always interesting to see the differences between the two. Apart from the heavier loss of life during the so called Great War, men then overwhelmingly joined the army with local regiments predominating. The 1939-1945 conflict saw a much wider variety of occupations in the armed forces, and Wilmslow men were spread throughout the services and theatres of war.

◄ **WILMSLOW**
*From the Railway
Viaduct 1897* 39601

This view across the River
Bollin shows 19th-century
building which resulted from
the expansion of the village
after the railway opened in
1842. This engineering
achievement obliterated the
Fittons' old manor house,
Bollin Hall, and also led to the
discovery of a number of
Bronze Age cremation urns.

◄ **WILMSLOW**
*The Memorial Gardens
c1955* W103003

The Memorial Gardens were
created on land cleared of
some rather dilapidated
cottages. This opening up of
the area continues; the
cottages to the left of the
George and Dragon by the
church went to make a new
car park for the pub, and now
the pub itself, despite its solid
classical appearance, has
closed and the land will be
redeveloped.

WILMSLOW
Grove Street 1897 39604

Wilmslow's main shopping street would contain all the shops needed by the community, including their links with the outside world, as the newspaper shop demonstrates in its adverts. The road dates from the 18th century; it is in fact the turnpike road. It only replaced Church Street as Wilmslow's main shopping street in the 1880s, when most of the shops in the photograph were built.

WILMSLOW
Grove Street c1955
W103006

This was Wilmslow's main
shopping street after the
war, and by 1955 the traffic
restrictions had started to
appear, with the no-waiting
signs at the top of the street.
Originally, Grove Street was
the turnpike road to
Manchester, and there was
a toll bar at this junction, a
great annoyance to
Wilmslow people who
objected to having to pay to
go down their main street.

► **WILMSLOW**
Bank Square Garden
c1955 W103007

At the other end of Grove Street, Bank Square took its name from the Union Bank of Manchester, with its fine clock and cupola. When the photograph was taken this was then Barclays' Bank but within 10 years that was to move to the corner at the top of Grove Street, and the old bank is now a pub.

◄ **WILMSLOW**
Station Road 1897
39605

Running up past the rectory on the right, this road would be taken by all the commuters going into Manchester from the station up on the right at the top. This was also the road out to Prestbury and Macclesfield. The junction with the old A34, the road to Manchester, is also known as Wilmslow Green.

◄ **WILMSLOW**
The Rectory 1897
39612

This double fronted
Georgian house exudes all
the comfortable status
that the Established
Church could expect at
the time it was built in the
late Georgian times. Too
big for modern clergymen,
it is now a restaurant, and
its old orchard contains
the town's leisure centre.

◀ **WILMSLOW**
Hawthorne Hall
1897 39613

The hall was built in 1698, but stylistically, the only sign of its date is the cupola and the classical hood over the central door, as this many-gabled house could have been built any time in the previous 10 years. But then, Cheshire has never been at the forefront of modern design. The hall passed through a number of hands, but for much of the 19th century it was a school.

◀ **WILMSLOW**
Pownall Hall 1897
39615

This was originally a plain five-bayed classical house dating from the 1830s, but in 1886 its new owner, the brewer Henry Boddington, asked William Ball to extend it. They commissioned The Century Guild to superintend the interior decoration, and the result is a remarkable Arts and Crafts house, with de Morgan tiles, Shrigley and Hunt windows, and a plethora of suitable inscriptions at every point.

▲ **WILMSLOW,** *Dean Row Chapel 1897* 39619

Dean Row chapel is one of a series of very similar Dissenter chapels built in North East Cheshire soon after the 1688 Toleration Act, testimony to the strong Nonconformist tradition that had developed in the county during the 17th century. The building was meant for hearing the word of God and originally the pulpit, being the most important feature in the interior, was sited in the middle of one of the long sides so that everyone could hear easily.

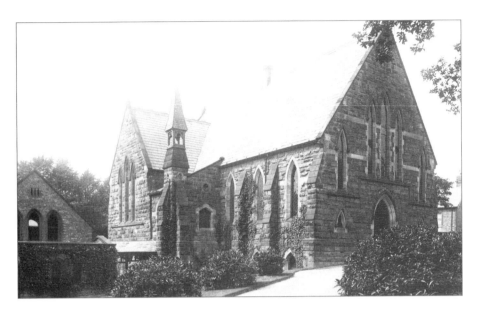

WILMSLOW
The Congregational Church 1897 39610

Situated on the road south to Alderley, this chapel would have served both communities. Built in the Gothic style in 1846-1847, it is typical of the solid prosperous church buildings that the new Nonconformist residents would expect to uphold their respectability.

WILMSLOW, *Lindow Church 1897* 39620

St John the Evangelist's Church, built in 1873-1874 by J W Beaumont, is a sign that the expanding population in Wilmslow had outgrown the original places of worship in the town, and with the creation of the new parish of Lindow to the south of Wilmslow, it needed something more. St John's came with its own school.

◀**WILMSLOW**
The View from Lime Walk 1897 39608

Lime Walk is part of the development of the Carrs, the old open pasture land that is still a great asset for the town. Many of the lines of old trees in the Carrs are the remnants of old field boundaries, but these trees were planted for their amenity value.

◄ **WILMSLOW**
Carrs Path c1955 W103009

The Carrs are part of the meadow land along the River Bollin that once provided pasture land for Wilmslow's residents. Now the scene of many a weekend football match, in the late 19th century it was where Wilmslow's washing was hung out to dry. The Bollin once powered a silk mill here, whose buildings later became a laundry that boasted that it returned everything except the dirt.

◄ **WILMSLOW**
Carrs Bridge c1955
W103000

Pownall Bridge over the River Bollin carries the public footpath that runs from Wilmslow along the river bank to Styal. It was built in 1800, after the Gregs raised the height of the weir at Styal and destroyed the old ford that took the road over to Pownall Hall.

WILMSLOW
The Romany's Caravan c1955 W103001

For a number of years during the Second World War, 'Romany', the Rev George Bramwell Evens, was a great favourite on Children's Hour with his nature talks, when he was often accompanied by his dog Raq. Evens' mother was a gypsy, and he and his wife restored this traditional caravan in the 1920s. After he died in 1943, Mrs Evens gave the van to Wilmslow, and Raq, who died in 1947, is buried beside it.

WILMSLOW
The Manchester Road c1965
W103014

Even in the 1960s the photographer must have risen very early to take this picture; although the cars were not yet controlled by lights, even then there was usually much heavier traffic on the main road into Manchester. The Bluebell Garage is still on the corner, although it now concentrates on selling expensive cars rather than petrol.

WILMSLOW, *Lindow Common c1955* W103010

This view looking south over Lindow Moss towards Alderley Edge, overlooks the area where Lindow Man, a first-century sacrificial victim, was found in 1984. A typical moss landscape of sedge and scruffy birch trees is in the foreground; beyond are some of the traditional peat cutters who were still working the area. The Lindow Common part of the moss is protected by an SSSI, but large areas are still being stripped of peat, despite local concerns about the loss of a fast diminishing habitat.

INDEX

NAMES OF SUBSCRIBERS

The following people have kindly supported this book by subscribing to copies before publication.

Abletts Chartered Accountants, Alderley Edge

David & Maureen Gardiner, Wilmslow

The Alsop Family, Alderley Edge

P W Gorman & Family, Wilmslow

The Barnett Family, Over Peover, Knutsford

Mr E & Mrs M Grange, Alderley Edge

Mr Martyn Beardwood, Handforth

Mr F & Mrs S Grange, Wilmslow

The Billington Family, Wilmslow

Mr D R & Mrs W Gray, Wilmslow

Eric Bonner

David & Maha Grice, Wilmslow

Peter John Bowker

Chris Guest

Marie Bramley

Mrs M J Hampson, Wilmslow

The Braybrooke Family, Wilmslow

Brian & Bridget Harris, Wilmslow

In memory of Vi & Ken Broadhurst, Wilmslow

In memory of R Hatherton, Wilmslow

John Brocklehurst

The Hawcroft Family, Wilmslow

Ray & Elaine Cross

William N Hawkhead, Handforth

The Cullom Family, Wilmslow

Jane Hay

Daniel & Andrew, Finsbury Way, Wilmslow

John & Joan Hillary, Beacon Lodge

Liza, Chris & Victoria Davies, Wilmslow

In memory of Jean Mavis Hulme from Dave

Peter Donoghue

In memory of Reginald & Margaret Hulme

In memory of Rae Doolin, Alderley Edge

Mr R & Mrs M P Hutchinson, Wilmslow

Mr E Edmondson, Wilmslow

Eirwen & Rob James, Prestbury

Peter & Lilian Falk, Wilmslow

Anne Jepson, Alderley Edge

Barbara J Foster

To my parents, Ernest & Mavis Johnson

Mr & Mrs R H Jones, Wilmslow

Peter P King, Wilmslow

Beverley Lake, Wilmslow

Mr J B & Mrs D Lennard, Wilmslow

J McDermott, Wilmslow

Amy, James, Ross & Thomas Meachin, Wilmslow

Ian, Jan, Ellie & Robbie Mecrow, Wilmslow

Mr B Michelson, Wilmslow

Mr & Mrs W M Nicol, Alderley Edge

In memory of Jessie & Charlie Norris

In memory of Victor O'Neill, Wilmslow

In memory of Norman Peacock, Wilmslow

Mr B J & Mrs W R Percival, Wilmslow

Cornelia L & Oliver J Pipping, Wilmslow

In memory of Alan Pugh, Wilmslow

Edith Randles, Alderley Edge

Mr N S Ratchford, Nether Alderley

Charles & Wendy Rowe, Wilmslow

David & Cynthia Russell

The Sabry Family, Alderley Edge

Robin & Mary Salmon, Wilmslow

Wendy Scott & Family, Bollington, Cheshire

Mr & Mrs Shaw and family, Wilmslow

Christopher Shenton

P A Simcock, Alderley Edge

A W & V A Smith, Moss Cottage, Alderly Edge, Ches.

Paul Vernon Angus Stott, Wilmslow

The Swinn, Heathcote and Sleath Families, Wilmslow

P S Tetlow of Wilmslow

Barbara Thompson, Wilmslow

Arthur Tinsley, Alderley Edge 1923

To David Tinsley, on his 50th Birthday

Peter J Upton, Wilmslow

Eric H Walker, Alderley Edge

Kathleen, Andrew & John Wallace, Alderley Edge

Brian & Kath Ward, Wilmslow

Barbara Welsh, Alderley Edge

FRITH PRODUCTS & SERVICES

Francis Frith would doubtless be pleased to know that the pioneering publishing venture he started in 1860 still continues today. Over a hundred and forty years later, The Francis Frith Collection continues in the same innovative tradition and is now one of the foremost publishers of vintage photographs in the world. Some of the current activities include:

Interior Decoration

Today Frith's photographs can be seen framed and as giant wall murals in thousands of pubs, restaurants, hotels, banks, retail stores and other public buildings throughout the country. In every case they enhance the unique local atmosphere of the places they depict and provide reminders of gentler days in an increasingly busy and frenetic world.

Product Promotions

Frith products are used by many major companies to promote the sales of their own products or to reinforce their own history and heritage. Frith promotions have been used by Hovis bread, Courage beers, Scots Porage Oats, Colman's mustard, Cadbury's foods, Mellow Birds coffee, Dunhill pipe tobacco, Guinness, and Bulmer's Cider.

Genealogy and Family History

As the interest in family history and roots grows world-wide, more and more people are turning to Frith's photographs of Great Britain for images of the towns, villages and streets where their ancestors lived; and, of course, photographs of the churches and chapels where their ancestors were christened, married and buried are an essential part of every genealogy tree and family album.

Frith Products

All Frith photographs are available Framed or just as Mounted Prints and Posters (size 23 x 16 inches). These may be ordered from the address below. From time to time other products - Address Books, Calendars, Table Mats, etc - are available.

The Internet

Already fifty thousand Frith photographs can be viewed and purchased on the internet through the Frith websites and a myriad of partner sites.

For more detailed information on Frith companies and products, look at these sites:

www.francisfrith.co.uk
www.francisfrith.com
(for North American visitors)

See the complete list of Frith Books at:
www.francisfrith.co.uk
This web site is regularly updated with the latest list of publications from the Frith Book Company. If you wish to buy books relating to another part of the country that your local bookshop does not stock, you may purchase on-line.

For further information, trade, or author enquiries please contact us at the address below:
The Francis Frith Collection, Frith's Barn, Teffont, Salisbury, Wiltshire, England SP3 5QP.
Tel: +44 (0)1722 716 376 Fax: +44 (0)1722 716 881 Email: sales@francisfrith.co.uk

See Frith books on the internet at www.francisfrith.co.uk